Bygone
DAGENHAM and RAINHAM

Rainham in the 1970s.

Bygone
DAGENHAM
and RAINHAM

Brian Evans

Phillimore

1992

Published by
PHILLIMORE & CO. LTD.
Shopwyke Hall, Chichester, Sussex.

ISBN 0 85033 831 X

Printed and bound in Great Britain by
BIDDLES LTD.
Guildford, Surrey

To Susan without whom ...
and to Colleen and Ron

List of Illustrations

Frontispiece: Rainham in the 1970s

Acknowledgements

The author would like to thank the following for all the help they have given with either the text or the illustrations: The Colchester and Essex Museum, The *Essex and Thurrock Gazette*, Ford Motor Company, Ms. Pamela Greenwood, Mr. R. Harris, the London Borough of Barking libraries, the London Borough of Redbridge libraries, The Governors and Trustees of the Passmore Edwards Museum, Trenthams, Mrs. S. Sherringham, Mr. Jack West and Mrs. Joan Wheal.

Introduction

In the Beginning

It has been shown that at a remote period the Thames was neither estuarine nor salt. Apparently at that time the land through which the river flowed was high enough to keep the sea at bay. In the marshes of Long Reach and also nearer to London, the topmost layer of the great mass of peat supported a forest of birch, elm, hazel, yew and several other varieties of tree. The yew is notoriously intolerant of water and cannot live in salt – yet the forest reached across the whole marsh, covering what is now Dartford, Rainham, Dagenham, Erith and nearby areas. The trunks of such trees have been discovered on either side of the river bank at sea level.

Many exciting finds which serve to throw light on the earliest inhabitants of Dagenham and Rainham have been made in the flood plain gravel about 20 ft. above sea level. The gradual rise from the alluvial levels of the old marshlands to this plain is a feature of these local haunts by the Thames of early man. Flint tools have been found in the Rainham area which span the Paleolithic (250,000 years ago), Mesolithic (*c.*8,000-4,000 B.C.) and Neolithic periods. The earliest earthwork in Rainham dates from the Neolithic period.

Some idea of the nature and environment of the early settlers can be gained from a site just across the river at Swanscombe. This site has yielded the earliest human remains to be found in this country. The Barnfield pit excavations, carried out between 1935-55, revealed skull fragments belonging to a young man in his early twenties, who lived approximately 250,000 years ago. Pollen remains indicate that the site was on a river estuary which opened out into the Thames. It would appear that the area comprised grass-covered mudflats divided by streams and edged by hazel scrub which continued inland as a mixed oak wood. This type of locale provided many of the materials needed by a hunting and food-gathering race. From bones found in the area it is known that the area abounded with elephants, rhinoceros, deer and horses, whilst the marshland provided birds and fish. The gravel terraces yielded flint for making chopper-core and flake tools. Later on, Swanscombe man, who appears to have been very advanced in skull type for his time – he was an early version of Homo Sapiens rather than the less human Homo Erectus which was more common at this time – was making fine handaxes of the Acheulian type.

It is likely that Swanscombe man and his contemporaries crossed the Thames on rafts or logs and produced the stone artefacts which were found on the north bank at Rainham. These tools show the progression in skill from the crude massive tools of the old stone age through to the less cumbersome implements of the middle period to the finely shaped blades of the new stone age.

The evidence of the area's animal life surfaced with the discovery of elephant teeth in the gravels; in 1964 at Sandy Lane, Aveley remains of the mammoth and straight-toothed elephant were found. Fluctuations in the area's climate 200,000 years ago is shown by the discovery of animal remains from both temperate and tropical zones.

The Neolithic ring ditch near Launders Lane, excavated in 1963 before gravel extraction started, surrounds a circular enclosure about 50 ft. in diameter which appears to have been prepared for some unknown ritual use. A pit in the middle of the ring probably contained the small crouched burial typical of these people. Within the pit fragments of middle and late Neolithic pottery were found together with some flint tools. Some of these items are now on view at the Passmore Edwards Museum in Stratford. The people connected with this enclosure were amongst Britain's first farmers, who were believed to have migrated from the Continent from about 4,000 B.C.

In 1922, during development in Dagenham, a very interesting wooden figure made from scotch fir was dug up from the marshes. This has since been called the Dagenham Idol. The figure has been dated to 2,350-2140 B.C., an age when even Thames man was involved in ritual practice. Several enclosures which could be connected with rituals have been discovered at Staines, Runnymede, Heathrow and Springfield in Essex.

A more settled period led to the emergence of the Bronze Age c.2,000 B.C., when first copper and then bronze tools and ornaments began to appear alongside stone and flint items. Pottery beakers have been found at Launders Lane and a complete beaker was found in the Gerpins Lane quarry.

In 1990, trenches dug by archaeologists working in advance of the Tesco development in Bridge Road, Rainham, revealed foreshore deposits near a former river or stream. Stake lines and wattle fences stood on this foreshore and there were pits cut into it with fire-cracked pebbles left behind. Spot and preliminary dating suggests that these trenches were made during the Bronze Age. Pottery from the late Iron Age was also discovered on this site in rubbish pits which were also full of animal bone. From the evidence we can deduce that towards the end of the prehistoric age the area was made up of a prosperous community of hunters, fishers and farmers who were domestically well-organised and able to defend themselves from attack.

At Moor Hall Farm, Rainham, archaeologists unearthed ten burial chambers dating from the late Bronze Age (approximately 8th-7th centuries B.C.). Small pits, each containing a burial urn, were placed side by side with pots meant for food and drink for the after-life. Flint flakes and blades were also included to act as tools. Thus a statement was made about life after death.

Moor Hall also yielded traces from the early Iron Age (6th - 3rd centuries B.C.) with the discovery of several circular and a number of semi-circular ones ditches. It is believed that these ditches marked the position of a settlement. The dig also revealed pottery and the remains of wall daub. It is almost certain that the settlement formed the nucleus of a farming community. Further excavation work at the same site uncovered a triple ditch enclosure – an important defensive feature from the late Iron Age (1st century B.C. -1st century A.D.).

Settlement of the Ruling People

It was not until after the period of Roman occupation that Rainham finally established a name and an identity. Although the Thames bank was not heavily settled by the Romans, they nevertheless left some reminder of their presence. When Moor Hall Farm was excavated between 1979-81 some remains of Roman activity were unearthed. The earliest finds were of a non-local pottery which had some late

Iron-Age features. Many ditches marking field boundaries and enclosures dating from the Roman era followed the pattern originally created in the late Iron Age. Although no definite settlement was found, there were small working areas and minor sand and gravel quarrying next to the farm. A second area to be excavated produced a Roman field system, dating mainly from the 2nd-4th centuries A.D. Some of the pottery that has been discovered has been dated to the 5th century. The extensive farming complex was abandoned at the end of the Roman period.

Pieces of a Romano-British food pot from Rainham's river bank confirm the antiquity of the Rainham Ferry site. Evidence of settlement in Roman Rainham is suggested by the discovery of part of a hand-worked corn grinding mill. This was found in what is now the Jewish cemetery, near White Post Corner. Dated c.A.D.150, this quern points to a settled farming family with a homestead, probably Romano-British. The quern and some pieces of superior pottery found near the cemetery would have had to have been imported from the Continent – this implies an affluent life-style. A second find of fragments of quern occurred to the west of Rainham, on the borders of Dagenham, at the aptly named Roman House on the Mardyke estate. These querns or handmills would usually be worked by the women of the settlement, by turning an upper circular moving stone around on a lower stationary one whilst feeding corn through a hole in the top stone in order to crush it between the two. The stones were usually made of lava from Germany.

In 1928 workmen recovered a stone coffin to the north of New Road, Rainham. When the lid was removed the bodies of two people lying head to foot were discovered. They were identified as Romans from the 4th century, one apparently a female. Buried with the bodies was a glass cup, and a small coin of Tetrarchus, who was Emperor of a short-lived splinter empire (A.D.267-273) which comprised Gaul, Spain, Britain and Germany. The site of the coffins does not indicate the site of a settlement, since under Roman law burials took place outside settlement boundaries. The corn-growing potential of the local Taplow gravel area would draw Roman farmers to the area. There is also the possibility that the Romans built the first river wall along the Thames.

At one time it was believed that there was a hiatus between the Roman and Saxon eras in Britain, but it now seems possible that the later Romano-British had a pact with the early Saxons, paying them to guard the shores.

The name 'Roegingaham' meaning 'settlement of the ruling people' occurs across the river in Kent and it is thought to be the origin of both Rainhams. Although a proper settlement has yet to be discovered, the activity of the Saxons in the Thameside wastes is known through excavation and early charters for Barking Abbey. In 1937 striking evidence of high Saxon culture came to light during gravel digging at Gerpins Farm with the discovery of a tremendous hoard of high quality grave goods. Shield bosses, spearheads, jewellery, pottery, and, unique in Britain, two glass drinking horns. These aroused a wealth of conjecture amongst antiquarians who debated the relationship of the drinking horns to examples from North Europe. Also found were two coins, brooches, rings, and bronze bound-wooden buckets. One coin, a golden solidus of Mauritius Tiberius (A.D.582-602) was set in a frame of gold wire for use as a pendant.

About seven miles to the east of Rainham is Mucking, the most important Saxon site in England, the dwellings, pottery and burial goods of which have been extensively investigated in recent years. Many of the investigations made here throw light upon the string of Saxon communities along the Thames.

Rainham's historian, Lewis, in his *History of Rainham*, deduces evidence of the Christianisation of the Saxons in the area alluding to the name Holy Bread field which can be traced back to the year 1294, and was still so-called in 19th-century tithe maps. This field, intriguingly, lay on the site of the Saxon burial ground and refers to a pre-Reformation endowment providing the Holy Loaf used at mass.

Two written records contribute to our understanding of Saxon Rainham. The Barking Abbey charter of A.D.697 grants land in Ricangahaam (a variation of Roegingaham). Domesday Book indicates a Saxon population of about three hundred and fifty. Such a population would seem to justify the provision of a Saxon church. A third clue lies in the ancient font bowl which was rediscovered quite recently. It was initially thought to be of Saxon origin but the Royal Commission on Historic Monuments pronounced it Norman. The basin is carved from rough hewn stone, on which two projecting pieces of stonework provide ornament and handle.

By the end of the Saxon era the land was divided among Alsi, a freeman, Aluard, and a priest, Lefstan. By the time of Domesday there were four manors in the area, as shown in the following table:

Domesday Figures

Manor	Southall		Berwick		Gerpins		Not identified (Launders)	
	1066	1086	1066	1086	1066	1086	1066	1086
Value	£6	£2	£1	£1	£10	£10	10s.	10s.
Villeins	8	8	4	5	12	12	–	–
Bordars	3	5	6	4	2	9	–	–
Serfs	4	0	2	0	5	4	–	–
Ploughs owned								
By men	3	3	2½	1	6	5	—	—
by demesne	4	0	2	2	3	2	½	0
Rouncies (horses)	–	–	3	4	–	1	–	–
Beasts (not plough animals)	–	–	14	11	–	–	–	–
Swine	–	–	6	24	–	20	–	–
Sheep	–	–	100	80	–	105	–	–
Beehives	–	–	–	12	–	–	–	–

In 1066 Rainham had a population of one hundred and ninety. Twenty years later this had only increased slightly to about two hundred and twenty living in 43 households. As a village lying off the major road routes, Rainham was not to grow appreciably larger for centuries to come. In the 17th century, for example, only 44 households are recorded.

It is difficult to be certain about the history of Rainham between 1086 and the 18th century because so little evidence exists.

The church of St Helen and St Giles in Rainham is unusual because it retains so much of its original Norman fabric, for example the massive piers and round-headed arches. The founder of the church was Richard de Lucy, the son-in-law of Henry II, the most important man in the kingdom after the king. The church was built between 1160-70.

It is recorded that by 1254 Southall Manor was owned by Roger de Crammaville, who made great attempts to drain the marsh. Excavations at Moor Hall Farm disclosed one of the few medieval ground features to be traced in modern times; this is a rectangular enclosure in the same field as the Neolithic ring ditch. Documentary evidence has proved the existence of other medieval houses in this area.

During the 15th and 16th centuries, the four manors were broken down into smaller holdings. This was due mainly to changes in the supply of labour. Before and during the 14th century the manorial system of forced labour was prevalent; the peasants owed the lord of the manor a certain number of days' work a year and in return were granted several manorial fields for their own use. This system began to break down during the later 14th century as personal service by the peasants was replaced by money payments, this money being used to pay hired labourers. Following the Black Death of 1349, when half of the population was wiped out, labour shortages made this system unprofitable. It became more common for the lord of the manor to hire out land to tenant farmers, who were responsible for paying rent and finding their own labour. In this way smaller farms came into being.

Daecca's Township

Roman presence in the Dagenham area is mainly inferred from their building of the Great Essex Road, which runs to the north of Dagenham through Chadwell Heath. In 1936, to the north of this road, in a field between Whalebone Lane North and Billet Lane, a coffin, carved from one solid block of sandstone, was discovered. The coffin was quite badly damaged, but there was still a skeleton inside it. Pottery vessels were also found nearby. Whilst the Becontree Estate was being constructed, near Dagenham village, three Roman items were discovered – a Castor Ware vase, a dark grey-ware bowl, and a grey-ware vase.

According to the Charter of Hodilred, which dates from A.D.692, Dagenham, along with Barking and Rainham, appears as one of the oldest place-names in Essex. The charter is an endowment by the Saxon prince, Hodilred, of the new Barking Abbey, and it cites the name of the land given as Deccanhaam. The village of Dagenham has, until relatively recently, always been linked with either Barking or Romford (it is included as part of Barking in Domesday Book). It was only during the 39 years 1926-65 that Dagenham ruled its own affairs, although it has figured throughout history as an individual community. There is a reference to Dagenham in the Pipe Roll of Richard I in 1195. Following this date frequent references occur which suggest that Dagenham had become a community of some importance. The connection of the village with Barking Abbey, no doubt provided a good administrative framework. This can be seen in the provision of a bridge, the famous Dagenham 'beam', originally a log or wide baulk of timber which had been specially hewn to span the river. The river flowing under this first bridge subsequently became known as the Beam. Some time before the reign of Henry VIII a stone bridge was built to replace the timber one. The river was an important feature in a document entitled a Perambulation of the Forest which dates from 1301. The jurors who undertook the walk along the eastern edge of the parish noted that the river had different names above and below the bridge:

> and from Hyleford (Ilford) straight by the same King's highway which leads towards Romford as far as a certain Cross set at the head of a certain lane called Wytheslane in the town of Havering (Romford); and from that Cross returning towards the south, by the hedge which is the boundary between the land of Gilbert Godebold of the fee of the Abbess of Berkyngg; and the land of John Atte Wythe of the fee of Havering, which edge is the boundary between the vills of Havering and Dakenham; and so by that hedge as far as the ditch of John le Franssch and Agnes atte Wythe of Dakenham. And by that ditch as far as the King's highway which leads from Hyleford to the Horned Monastery (Hornchurch), as a certain water runs across the same highway, which water is called Wythendenbroke, and is the boundary between Havering and Dakenham. And from that water as far as a certain place called la Berwe [la bruyère -the Heath] with all the piece of land in which is the aforesaid place called la Berwe [the Heath], as the boundary extends between the vills of Havering and Dakenham as far as a certain stream of water called the Borne, which water runs down from a certain spring called Haveringwelle as far as a certain place called Dakenhambeem, and from that place as far as the line of the water of the Thames by a certain ditch called Markedyke, between Havering and Dakenham.

Various legal documents, such as Feet of Fines, Proceedings in Chancery and Inquisitions after Death all mention Dagenham.

A matter of great importance for the inhabitants of the village was the repair of Thames wall, a structure, which in part dated back to Roman and Saxon times. The antiquarian, W. Glenny, believed that 'the embanking and draining which now preserve the meadows seem to have been done by Kings of the Saxon period because many of them go by the name of the King's Meads, some being granted to the several parishes as common all the year, or common after mowing time'. If the walls were not well maintained, valuable agricultural land was flooded. So important was the wall that some documents record Royal appointments to a local commission for the Thames wall. In the reigns of Richard II and Edward IV patents were passed for the repair of the wall. From the time of Henry VIII the body responsible for the upkeep of the wall was known as the Dagenham and Havering Commission of Sewers, and under Royal Warrant it controlled both the Thames wall and the banks of the river.

Other documents refer to the manors, the founding of the parish and the building of the church, the foundations of which date from the 13th century. In 1800 the church tower collapsed, only three years after Royal consent had been sought to collect money to rebuild it: 'The Parish church of Dagenham aforesaid is a very ancient pile of Gothic building and by the length of time is become so ruinous in many parts that it hath been with extreme danger ... that Parishioners have ventured to assemble therein ... from North and South sides of the Tower in particular are split from top to bottom'. In 1529 the rood of the church had gained great sanctity and money was left in a Kentish yeoman's will for a visit to made to 'the Rode of Rest at Dagnham'. In 1553 Heywood, in his poem 'The Four P's', refers to the 'good rood' of Dagenham, a reference perhaps to the miracles ascribed to the rood. In 1563, after the Reformation, an inventory was drawn up of all the church goods. Many of the vestments and silver were sold leaving only 'four bells and a Sanctus bell and a rood loft'.

Many of the older buildings in Dagenham were photographed before 1920, prior to the building of the Becontree Estate. Some of them were demolished during the construction of the estate, or have since been lost; however, some memory of them is retained through place-names or parts of buildings which have been preserved or incorporated into other houses. Some buildings bear the name of old Dagenham families. Eastbrooks is first mentioned in 1284, Frizlings (later Frizlands) was renamed when it was purchased by the de Fristling family in 1303, although the family actually came to Dagenham in 1284. Gale Street Farm was named after the family of Richard de Gal, who is also recorded as being in Dagenham in 1284. In 1556 Hunters Hall was known as Howmans, after a family known as Hallman. It was later renamed after the Hunter family and was referred to as Hunters Hall by 1779. Foxlands is a 15th-century name which has survived. Bennetts Castle Farmhouse was built in 1618, although Castle Field was known as such as early as 1440.

Many of the smaller cottages built on the marshland became so integrated with their surroundings that it was forgotten how old they were. For example, White Cottage at Five Elms dated from before the Tudor period. In addition Tan Yard Cottages, Rainham Road, Vine Cottage, Wood Lane, Joyner's Cottages, Hunters Hall Cottages, Grays's Cottages, Oxlow Lane and Rose Cottages in Scottes Lane were all very old. Many cottages of the most primitive construction, often without proper foundations and built of non-durable materials, were to survive well into the 20th century and were even to be found in odd corners of the massive Becontree Estate.

Perhaps it was wise to spend sparingly on accommodation when it was never certain what disaster might overtake the land. On 20 October 1707 at Sandcreek in the Dagenham Level a small trunk sluice in the river wall, which a Mrs. Susan Uphill had neglected to have repaired, blew out, causing the collapse of a 14ft. wall. The river immediately came through and 1,000 acres of marshland was flooded. For a variety of reasons no preventative measures were carried out until December 1715, when a good engineer was found in John Perry. He faced the mammoth task of closing a gap which was by now 400ft. wide and still widening. In addition the silt washing out into the Thames was forming a bank which looked likely to close the Port of London. Ignoring political obstruction, slanderous attacks by those who had failed, unscrupulous workers and dishonest contractors, Perry managed to close the breach in June 1720 after two previous efforts had been unsuccessful. The landscape of this area already bore the marks of previous incursions of the river, most notably in the shape of Dagenham 'Gulph', an irregular-shaped lake; the family of Elizabeth Fry had a cottage hidden away on its shores. The lake also became a favourite place for fishing, both amongst locals and visitors from London, continuing as such until the 20th century.

It was believed impossible to develop this stretch of the waterfront, but the firm of Samuel Williams transformed hundreds of acres of marsh into an industrial site, the arrival of the Ford Motor Company in 1929 being the culminating factor.

Memories of Yesterday's Dagenham and Rainham

In 1912 a writer described Dagenham thus: 'Dagenham itself is surrounded by cornfields and market gardens. The soil is exceedingly fertile and being flat is easily worked. The village is quaint and old world, many of its houses being boarded with gable roofs'.

Ryan MacMahon, a doctor who opened a private practice in December 1925 on the new L.C.C. estate at Dagenham, saw the town in rather less picturesque light when describing an interesting spare-time activity: 'We formed a rat-hunting club and held meets on the enormous garbage dumps beside the river near Rainham. Two fellow-practitioners, a dentist and the Roman Catholic padre were keen members of the hunt. The pack consisted of a Great Dane, an Irish Setter, and a Spaniel: a more inappropriate trio could hardly have been selected with malice aforethought, but we had lots of fun ...'.

In January 1948 a Mrs. Maiden of Rainham, who was then 90 years old, reminisced about her life in Rainham and the changes that had occurred:

The Clock Tower erected as a memorial to Rainham men who fell in the 1914-18 War now forms the centre of the town and is used as a terminus for the Barking, Romford, Hornchurch and Tilbury bus services. Each morning and evening the centre is thronged with factory workers, embarking and disembarking from the buses and even the middle-aged workers remember the duck pond which was filled in to provide the site of the Clock Tower.

The centre was then known as the Green and the grass verges of the pond provided a playground for many who are now grown up. The bank, the old post office, a coffee shop, two or three general shops, three public houses, a line of cottages and the big house then comprised the centre of the village around the Green.

The big house was a country mansion of which the last resident was Mr. Sturgess, a Rainham solicitor. As an extremely old building it is associated with the interesting legend that a smuggler's tunnel runs from its cellar to the *Crown Inn* on the riverside, a mile and a half away, in a direct line. To the end of the Great War it was a common sight to see the wagons of local farmers driving down to Swann's wharf just opposite the clock tower to meet the barges laden with fertilizers.

Swann's wharf is now discarded but barges still carry timber up the creek as far as Newman's timber yard opposite the *Bell Hotel*. Farmers wagons also congregated in those days when setting out with produce for Covent Garden. Twenty years ago there was such a glut of potatoes in the Rainham area that they were being given away by the sack. This seemingly incredible harvest was particularly heavy on a piece of land known as Brights' Farm – the forty acres. Residents were given permission to go on the land and pull up as many potatoes as they wanted.

Many of the old memories are associated with the Ingrebourne River which flows by the town. Twenty years ago traffic to Rainham had to cross the river over a quaint old wooden bridge, each year the floods roared down the weed-choked river to inundate the nearby houses.

To the north of Rainham was Damyns Hall Farm, Aveley Road which was owned by Farmer Vellacott and later tenanted by his former horseman, George Paveley. Three generations of Paveleys worked the farm from 1887. Mrs. Joan Wheal remembers the last years of the farm building, which is believed to date back to the 16th century. The south front was described as:

having a four course brick string course dividing the ground and first floors, also a parapet and gable to the south in which is a blocked window. Moulded brick cornice and another blocked window below the cornice at the west corner. The south wing is gabled, the south face being modern rebuilding. The west face has two gables, one to the main wing, the south gable is smaller. Below the south gable is a short length of similar moulded cornice.

A remarkable feature of the building was the original south entrance door which had a heavy chamfered square head and a frame that was divided into nine parts by moulded horizontal and vertical ribs. The door was also studded with square nails.

In its last days, part of the house was held up by scaffolding and one wing had already collapsed. However, the fascination of living in such an old building which was still in use as a working farm was great. Mrs. Wheal remembers the wind whistling through the beams during windy nights and there were many other noises to be heard. The farmhouse still contained 16 rooms, amongst them a huge kitchen, and a butler's pantry with a stone slabbed floor. A well, which was said to never fail, was situated below the main kitchen, but approached via outside steps. The farm was eventually sold and, in 1965, after the family had moved it was destroyed by fire.

Dagenham in the 1920s became largely synonymous with the Becontree housing estate, the largest housing estate in Europe, and also with the Ford Motor Works.

The area was seen by outsiders as an area of monolithic housing and class structure. The local inhabitants knew that the picture was much more complicated and interesting.

In the modern era Dagenham has produced a large number of sportsmen and entertainers, such as Jim Peters and Dudley Moore. Others like Hardy Amies grew up in the district. So it has produced its own kind of excellence.

The schools and libraries in the district were equal to the best in Britain and assisted in this growth to maturity in this town which grew from its isolated village origins.

Rainham's development has been more sporadic; it has gradually abandoned its village status. This impetus was partly through the efforts of weekend homebuilders in the 1920s and '30s who bought plots of land and visited them regularly, slowly building up the structure, at the same time using their visits as a holiday break from the work routine. Other people came to more permanent developments which housed workers in the different industries in Ferry Lane; most of these eventually became part of the Murex works. Particularly since the Second World War many commuters have chosen Rainham as a home because its railway line terminates at Fenchurch Street station in the heart of the City.

In the Beginning

Interesting Links with the Past Unearthed

Interesting relics of Rainham's past were uncovered this week when a five-man team from the Ministry of Works completed a three-weeks-old investigation into the earthworks ina field near Launders Lane. A quantity of both Neolithic and medieval pottery has been discovered and it is thought that the site was used around 1,800 B.C. for sacrificial rites and religious ceremonies. The excavations have not been made public before for fear of ivasion by sightseers.

The story of the discovery began some months ago when an aerial photograph of the area was taken by Dr. J. K. St Joseph, of Cambridge University. Because these historic trenches hold more water than the clay surrounding them, the crops which grow from them show greener from an aerial view, and in this case, indicated the existance of a circular trench and many ditches which formed an enclosure.

A little time after this, the owners of the land, Hoveringham Gravel Company, removed the topsoil of the area and revealed more plainly the site. Three weeks ago a team from the Ministry of Works and Public Buildings came to Rainham to dig the site expecting it to date from the Iron Age. When, however, the first trenches were opened, it was found that they were medieval in origin and later dated as being 1,200 A.D.

Led by Dr. I. E. Smith and Mr. Derek Simpson, M.A., the team went on to examine the circular ditch, fearing this too would be medieval. After careful digging for some days and examination of the pottery pieces found, it was declared, however, that this circle was prehistoric and seemed to have been used as a place of worship.

The discovery also of Neolithic pottery in the ditch has caused a review of previous dating of this pottery, as Dr. Smith said ... 'The discovery of such a prehistoric monument in these conditions is unique in my experience ... In the circular ditch we discovered various flints and pieces of beaker shard, which have proved to be Neolithic. The medieal pottery was much the same as we find anywhere else. An interesting feature of the site is that the prehistoric and the medieval are so close together, although it would probably be the stream nearby that attracted settlements'.

1. Picture from the *Essex and Thurrock Gazette* of the Launders Lane earthwork.

2. The Dagenham Idol, a wooden figure carved from scotch fir and found in the marsh in 1922. Radiocarbon dating has placed this figure between 2350 - 2140 B.C.

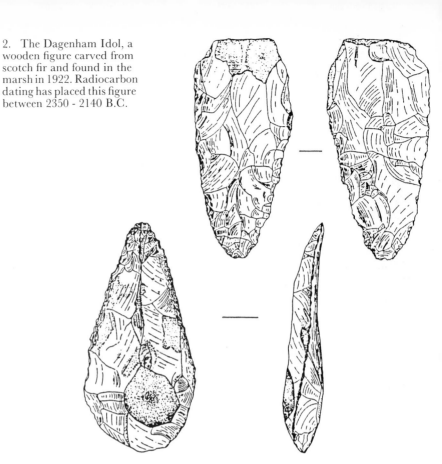

3. Stone-age tools found at Berwick Road and thought to date from the old and new stone ages.

4. Sarsen stone at Moor Hall, 1964. These sandstone boulders are to be found deep below the Essex clays or in the beds of its rivers. It is thought that the stones were often placed in groups in ancient times to act as religious areas and to mark burial sites. Several have been incorporated into the walls of Christian churches when they succeeded Pagan places of worship.

5. Discovery of the bones of a mammoth and a straight-tusked elephant near Sandy Lane, Aveley, in August 1964.

6. In 1928 a Roman coffin containing the remains of two bodies was discovered near to Rainham in South Hornchurch. The figures, one apparently a woman, were lying head to foot and dated from the third century A.D. The dress of the workmen is now itself a period piece.

Settlement of the Ruling People

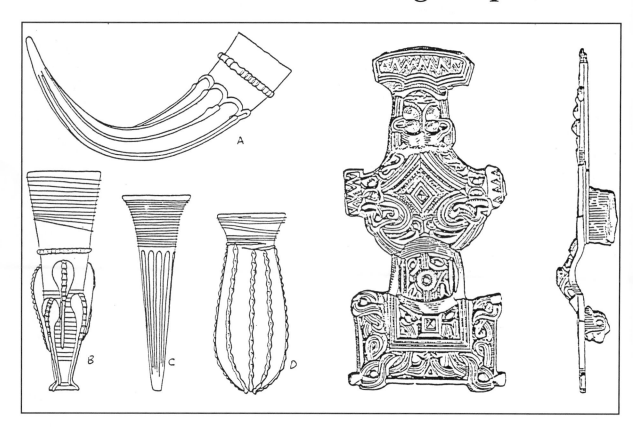

7. (*Above left*) One of two Saxon drinking horns dug up in 1937 at Gerpins Farm, Rainham. Unfortunately the original circumstances of the find meant that it was not properly written up, but the objects found with the horn were all photographed, which has led to later evaluation. This drawing of the attractive green vessel in the shape of a cattle horn is compared with other types of glass with similar decoration: a. the Rainham horn; b. claw-beaker, Taplow, Bucks.; c. cone beaker, Kempston, Beds.; d. bag beaker, Faversham, Kent.

8. (*Above*) A gilt bronze Saxon square-headed brooch, with zoomorphic designs, was also found in the 1937 hoard. Animal shapes and downward-biting animal heads form part of the complicated pattern. Many brooches of this type have surfaced in the Cambridge area but all show the influence of a Kentish-type artistry.

9. (*Left*) Bronze-bound wooden bucket with silvered vandykes, (strenghtening plates in the form of a triangle), from a male Saxon inhumation at Mucking, only a few miles along the Thames from Rainham. The buckets from Mucking, one of the most important Saxon archaeological sites in Britain, are better-preserved than those found at Gerpins Farm in Rainham in 1937.

10. The beautiful Norman priest's door on the south side of the chancel of Rainham church.

11. Inside St Helen and St Giles c.1930, showing the round arches and various features of Norman work as well as later alterations.

12. Close-up of the Norman capitals to the respond of the north arcade. Photographed by Mr. J. Salmon in the early 1930s.

13. The remarkable parish chest dating from the 15th or 16th century with lid raised. This particular chest was originally a 'travelling' or standard chest with four carrying handles (still intact). The body is covered in gesso or plaster of an orange-red colour, patches of which remain. The lid is protected by black leather.

14a. Looking through the railings, themselves work of superior craftsmanship, to the porch of Rainham Hall in the 1930s. The building beyond is the lodge which was probably built before the Hall.

14b. Garden front of the Hall. The stone garden vases are contemporary with the Hall.

15. A very old photograph of Back Street and the smithy. Back Street is now Upminster Road South. The churchyard wall may be seen on the right. The site of the smithy was in later times occupied by Mr. Cutbush, the florist.

16. The rear view of Redberry, as is often the way, displays an older image than the frontage onto the Broadway. The projecting bay window is once supposed to have overlooked a 'Redberry Wharf'.

17a.   Damyns Hall was an old farmhouse destroyed by fire in 1965. Part of the left-hand side of the house had collapsed and was shored up by wooden beams. The remaining portion was used by the farmer's family until a short time before the fire. The Hall had many fascinating features, such as an unfailing well, situated under the house, reached by external steps.

17b.   This ancient, nine-battened door leading into Damyns is probably the original. The house was believed to have been built in the 17th-century on the site of an earlier structure.

18.   The second Gerpins manor house was built in the late 19th century opposite the original building. This was also demolished during the extensive gravel winning processes on this site where the Saxon burial hoard was uncovered. The manor appears in Domesday Book. John and Laurence Jarpeville, who came from the town of Gerpenville on the Seine in France, gave the manor its name in the 13th century.

19.   Ayletts Farm, Warwick Lane, now demolished. The left-hand portion was built in the 17th century. The name comes from the family of John Ayleward who appears in the Feet of Fines records of 1339. On the 1777 map of Essex it is called Elliotts.

20. A distant view of Rainham from the flood plain of the Ingrebourne marshes at the end of the 19th century.

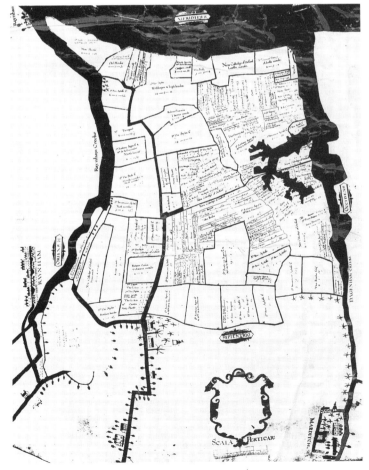

21. Map of Hornchurch Marsh showing landowners and field names, *c*.1630. Being an old map, south is at the top (towards the Thames). Rainham village can be seen on the left and Marditch or Mardyke Farm is portrayed as an important estate by Dagenham creek on the right-hand side. Frog Island, at the the mouth of the Ingrebourne, is here identified as New Hooke as opposed to Old Hooke further west.

22a.   Rainham creek. Sailing boats and barges regularly used the creek in the 19th and early 20th centuries. This picture shows the lighthouse or beacon at Great Coldharbour in 1962.

22b.   Barge on the creek at anchor.

22c. Barge moving up creek.

22d. Maldon barge loading with logs.

23. 'Holy bread' field was the site of the Gerpins Saxon burial and later provided the holy loaf used at pre-Reformation Mass. Gravel working destroyed it.

24. The Broadway before the war memorial was built. On the left Redberry's frontage shows its distinctive late 18th-century character with its Georgian doorway and leaded fanlight. In the centre is the old *Angel Inn* which was demolished in 1905. On the right is a wagon-load of hay.

25. Dovers farmhouse (Little Dovers) which is now the presbytery of La Salette church.

26. Remains of Dovers moat. This surrounded Great Dovers, the ancient manor house, formerly on the site of the present *Albion* public house. The name came from the family of Philip de Dover, which originated from the Kent fortress town, and whose burial slab is in the church.

27a. Stool made from pieces removed from Wennington church pulpit when it was altered.

27b. Wennington church, showing the Norman doorhead of the priest's door.

27c. Excavation of the nave foundations of the church. A skeleton was found in the recess of the north-east angle.

28. Great Coldharbour,
Wennington – a lonely riverside
farm demolished *c*.1920. In
1848 an 'Independent Minister'
and farmer lived here named
Henry Cooke Bourne. He died
in 1855 and is commemorated
on an obelisk at the church
bearing the initials 'H.C.B.'.

29. Before the school adjoining
Wennington church was
constructed in 1876, this
timbered and thatched cottage
in Church Lane, which
belonged to the churchwardens,
served as the school house. The
building has now been
demolished.

30. Lenthorpe House, Wennington in 1961. It was also known as Leventhorpe; the name was recorded as far back as 1544.

31. Willow Farm, Wennington in 1963 – once called Scripps. William Walker, who lived here in the 19th century was a firm supporter of the 'Fancy' or Noble Art.

32. South Hall, Wennington. The manor of South Hall is recorded in Domesday Book as belonging in Saxon times to Alsi (Alsius), a freeman. In the 14th century the manor was held by the Prior of the Hospital of St John of Jerusalem.

33. Wennington Hall. In 1851 James Hall was the farmer here with 10 labourers working on 250 acres.

34. A view of Rainham earlier this century, taken from the elevated platform of the railway station, shows the medieval layout of the village. Centuries had passed without disturbing the simplicity of the plan.

Daecca's Township

35.   Old Dagenham parish church of SS Peter and Paul as it looked *c.*1770. It was originally built in the 12th-13th centuries at the behest of the Abbess of Barking. The south aisle was added in the 15th century and is mentioned in the will of John Valentyne, the vicar, who died in 1475: 'My bodie to be beryed in ye newe ile or chapele of Seynt Petry's Church in Dakenham'.

36. Sir Thomas Urswick, as depicted on a brass in Dagenham church. One of Dagenham's most powerful lords, he originally came from a Westmorland family, being elected Common Serjeant to the Corporation of London in 1453, and a Recorder in the next year. He was a learned and able lawyer, but an ambitious and unscrupulous man in pursuit of the main chance. He played a leading role in the deposition from the throne of Henry VI, while helping to establish Henry's rival, Edward IV in his stead. Note the interesting 'butterfly' head-dress fashion of his lady.

37. The most imposing monument in the church is that to the memory of Sir Richard Alibon. He is shown lifesize, wearing his judicial robes and holding a roll of parchment. His wife carries a clasped book. He was made a judge in 1687, the year he bought a house on the north side of Dagenham, opposite to that of the Comyns family. The house was known as Camms and was approached through an avenue of trees; it was pulled down in the 19th century. Alibon died, it was said, of fright, thinking he was about to be prosecuted for treason for accepting an office from which he was disqualified as a Catholic.

38. Dagenham church shown here rebuilt after the collapse of the tower one Sunday morning in December 1800. Fortunately, because the parson was late, the congregation had not been able to enter. Only the chancel and a small chapel from the original edifice were saved from the wreckage.

39. In this picture the artist Bennett Bamford makes the rebuilt church blend harmoniously with the other buildings of the village. A variety of building materials has been used, including stone, brick and timber, and the artist makes good use of the contrasts.

40. Looking eastwards along Dagenham's main street, 1889. The stone bears the legend F.B.D., 1658 and is set into the house on the right of the picture.

41. Dagenham church interior, c.1905. The iron screen leads to the ancient chapel. The pulpit is newer and the wall monuments have been resited on the right.

42. Dagenham as a tourist spot, *c.*1931. The shop on the right provided teas for the visitor. Note the gas lamps.

43. Parsloes Mansion.

44. The interior of Parsloes, 1878. The picture shows a panelled room with portraits of the Fanshawes, which are now at Valence House, and a cheerful fire.

Anno Regni
GEORGII
REGIS

Magna Britannia, Francia, & Hibernia,

SEPTIMO.

At the Parliament Begun and Holden at *Westminster*, the Seventeenth Day of *March*, Anno Dom. 1714. In the First Year of the Reign of our Sovereign Lord *GEORGE*, by the Grace of God, of *Great Britain, France,* and *Ireland*, King, Defender of the Faith, &c.

And from thence Continued by several Prorogations to the Eighth Day of *December*, 1720. Being the Sixth Session of this present Parliament.

G R

LONDON,

Printed by *John Baskett*, Printer to the Kings most Excellent Majesty, And by the Assigns of *Thomas Newcomb*, and *Henry Hills*, deceas'd. 1721.

45. An Act of Parliament passed in 1721, during the reign of George II. This shows the title page of the Act and a clause for relief of Captain John Perry in his efforts to stop the breach at Dagenham and repair the damage to navigation in the Thames. It raises 'several duties on Coals and Shipping'.

Clause for Relief of Captain John Perry concerning Dagenham Breach.

And whereas in and by an Act passed in the Twelfth Year of Her late Majesty Queen Anne, Intituled, An Act for the speedy and effectual preserving the Navigation of the River of *Thames*, by stopping the Breach in the Levels of *Havering* and *Daggenham*, in the County of *Essex*; and for ascertaining the Coal-Measure, several Duties on Coals and Shipping were granted, and Trustees therein appointed to apply and dispose of the same, to the stopping the said Breach, in such manner as they should think most convenient: And whereas on the Twenty fifth Day of January, One thousand seven hundred and fifteen, the said Trustees contracted with Captain John Perry for stopping the said Breach for the Sum of Twenty five thousand Pounds, and to maintain the same for Three Years after stopt, or in case of Accidents, to make good the Damage; upon Condition that if such Sum was not sufficient, they would recommend him to Parliament: And whereas the said John Perry hath effected and performed the said Work according to his Contract, the Charge and Expence whereof hath amounted to the Sum of Forty thousand four hundred seventy two Pounds, Eighteen Shillings, and Eight Pence Three Farthings, of which Sum several of the Creditors of the said John Perry, to whom he is indebted for Premiums, are willing to remit to the said John Perry the Sum of Five thousand nine hundred forty seven Pounds, and five Shillings, which being deducted out of the said Forty thousand four hundred seventy two Pounds, Eighteen Shillings, and Eight Pence Three Farthings, there will be still wanting Nine thousand five hundred and five Pounds, Thirteen Shillings, and Eight Pence Three Farthings, over and above the Twenty five thousand Pounds agreed to be paid by the said Trustees to the said John Perry, to enable him to defray the Charge and Expence of the said Work: And whereas several Security Bonds have been entered into to the said Trustees for the Repayment of several Sums of Money, in case the said John Perry should not have performed his said Contract for stopping the said Breach, and also for maintaining the Work for Three Years after the same should be stopped: And some Doubts having arisen about the Commencement of the said Three Years, Be it therefore Enacted by the Authority aforesaid, That the said Trustees be hereby impowered and required, out of the Money collected or to be collected by Virtue of the said Act, to pay and satisfie to the said John Perry, his Executors, Administrators, or Assigns, the further Sum of Fifteen thousand Pounds. And it is hereby Declared, That the Three Years for which the said John Perry was or is to maintain the said Work, did commence from the Nineteenth Day of July, One thousand seven hundred and eighteen, being the Day on which the Breach was first reputed to be stopt according to his Contract, the Damage that hath since happened being now sufficiently repaired; Any thing in the said Act of the Twelfth Year of Her late Majesty Queen Anne to the contrary in any wise notwithstanding:

Anno Regni Septimo Georgii Regis.

46. Valence House, looking towards the north-west. This picture was taken on 21 March 1930.

47.   Eastbrook Farm, Bull Lane, Dagenham. This is a rear view of the farm taken in October 1930. The house was demolished in May 1931.

48. Eastbrook Farm, October 1930.

49. The interior of Eastbrook Farm. This is a detail of an upper floor partition showing its construction of rushes and daubed plaster. The picture dates from the time of demolition.

50. Ancient walls and doors in an upper room of Eastbrook Farm.

51. Stacey's Cottage, Becontree Heath, October 1930.

52. Sheepcotes, Billet Lane, Dagenham, 11 October 1930.

53. A rather primitive cottage in
Eastbrook End Road, Dagenham,
photographed on 9 May 1931.

54. Clay Cottages, Marston Avenue
originally served as Tudor farm-
labourers' dwellings and therefore are
probably about five hundred years old. In
January 1962 this cottage, although
'improved' and with an upper floor
inserted, with a tile as opposed to a
thatched roof, stood condemned to be
demolished. Similar cottages in Rush
Green had been demolished in 1934.

55. The Fry family holidaying at Dagenham Breach Cottage, 1825-26.

56. A sale notice for a freehold house in Dagenham, 1874.

57. Looking down Crown Street in 1910. The cottage on the right acts as an office for Bale, General Contractor. Further down the street a barber's pole projects from the line of buildings which date from various centuries.

58. This drawing of Crown Street dates from earlier than the previous photograph, and some of the same buildings may be seen.

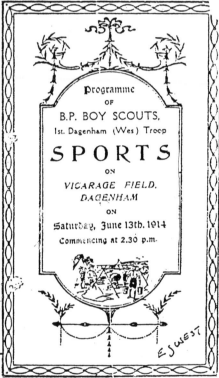
59. Shops advertising in the Scouts Sports Programme, June 1914.

Beer and Skittles

Post Office, Dagenham.

60. Bull Street, the *Bull Inn* and the post office, *c.*1905. Also to be seen are some rather cramped cottages and a cart loaded with sacks. The ladies are obviously very surprised that any photographer should be interested in this scene.

61. Further back along the street, at about the same date, pedestrians wait expectantly for the camera to do its work. W. Howgego's cycle and motorcycle shop was soon to launch into selling and providing for the needs of automobiles, well before the name of Ford became inseparable from Dagenham.

62. Looking up Crown Street, *c*.1910. This picture shows a residential area, with large houses surrounded by gardens.

63. Bull Street is really a main through road, but only two cyclists provide any evidence for this. A workman plods towards the camera, walking in the gutter, and numerous children are to be seen on the pavement, no doubt enjoying the novelty of seeing a professional photographer.

64. Inns and taverns frequently provided the only opportunity for relaxation for working men. Shown here are two Edwardian inns: *The Chequers* (above) was on the main Barking to Dagenham road and so well placed for farm workers. The *Robin Hood* (below) seen here *c.*1910 in a rural setting, was soon to become part of the built-up Becontree area.

65. Members of Dagenham Brass Band pose proudly in front of Dagenham Vicarage, *c*.1920.

SACRED

TO THE MEMORY OF
GEORGE CLARK
LATE A POLICE CONSTABLE
OF THE K DIVISION OF
METROPOLITAN POLICE
WHO WAS INHUMANLY AND
BARBAROUSLY MURDERED
IN A FIELD AT EASTBROOK
END, IN THIS PARISH,
WHILST ON DUTY, ON THE
NIGHT OF THE 20TH OR THE
MORNING OF THE 30TH JUNE
1846,
AGED 20 YEARS.

⬥

HIS UNIFORM GOOD
CONDUCT GAINED HIM
THE RESPECT OF ALL
WHO KNEW HIM, AND HIS
MELANCHOLY END WAS
UNIVERSALLY DEPLORED.

66. In 1840 Dagenham became the farthest district to be covered by the Metropolitan Police. Unfortunately a certain amount of corruption existed in those days, and it would appear, although it has never been proved, that George Clark, a young constable, was killed for refusing to cooperate with his fellow officers who were probably involved in a smuggling operation.

But I tell you 'tis no use your coming here there is no property left on my land but the old scare crow – no one will steal him I should think

EXTENSION of the NEW POLICE

67. This incident was only one of many difficulties experienced in the early days of national policing. Public opinion was not generally in favour and many cartoons were published guying the force, such as this one of 1840.

68. Dagenham police station was initially located in an old house in Bull Lane. The second station, seen here, was used for over a century, being vacated by the force in 1963.

69. Dagenham police officers line up for the camera in 1938.

70.   The 1st Dagenham (Wesleyan) Scouts in 1911. The movement was still in its infancy, with troops of any age being accepted, since the Cubs had yet to be formed. A stave was an essential part of the gear and a South African colonial type of uniform was worn, deriving from Baden-Powell's experience in the Boer War.

71.   A great benefactress of the Dagenham area was doctor's wife, Mrs. Prosser-Evans, seen here leading the Dagenham Clinic outing to Clacton on 26 July 1923. She is standing at the front of the charabanc which formed part of S. Palmer's fleet from Romford.

72. Sterling's factory football team seen here with their trophies from the 1919-20 season.

73. Early stars of Dagenham cricket team.

E. ARNOLD

A. E. RELF

FIELDER

KNIGHT

74. A children's fancy dress tableau organised by Mrs. Prosser-Evans to celebrate the Empire. Her work in Dagenham was once legendary, her benevolence necessary in the days before the welfare state.

75.   Two views of the Dagenham Vicarage garden party of 20 June 1912. The garden party brought together many members of the community and various events and games were organised such as the ladies slow cycling race seen below.

76.   The open wastes of Becontree Heath, seen here in the early years of this century. The area was unenclosed and provided an excellent playground for children. Unfortunately few drains meant that large pools of water gathered on the lower ground, sometimes inconveniently near the *Three Travellers* inn, as seen in this photograph.

77.   This later photograph shows some signs of development on the heath. A pile of gravel lies on the roadside waiting to be used. Nanny Goat Common was shortly to be enclosed and developed.

78. A rare local cartoon shows the heath and the *Three Travellers* in 1820. This public house is the oldest in the area. The central character in the cartoon is Benjamin Wasey Sterry, a local lawyer who held many important offices in this part of Essex. A scandal concerning the Heath is alluded to. Mr. 'Scruty' on the right stands for scrutineer of justice. The cartoon was issued by Mr. Tipper, a Romford bookseller, who had been deprived by Sterry of the appointment of postmaster.

79. The famous Rainham dump, to which much of London's rubbish was brought, seen here in the 1930s. It had a reputation for being a horrific rat-infested feature of the landscape, yet the men who worked on it and local people had many tales of incredible treasures found there.

80. Flooding in Bridge Road, Rainham. Looking from the Red Bridge towards the village and showing the cottages, known locally as Flood Row, since they were frequently flooded.

81. Locals, staff and regulars of the *Three Crowns* inn, seen here on the river bank on 20 August 1899. This area was once known as Rainham Ferry and supported a thriving community at the end of the 19th and beginning of the 20th centuries. Note the potman on the left, a man believed to be a gamekeeper standing by the window, and assorted characters and children. There are at least two good ratting dogs in the picture.

82. Rainham-on-Thames holiday resort, 1921. The *Three Crowns* building dates back to 1830. For four centuries a succession of alehouses has stood on this spot, at the mouth of Rainham creek. This was a place of call for the Long Ferry, which plied between Gravesend and London. During the 1920s and '30s East Londoners and other day-trippers began to frequent this spot.

83. In 1923 Mr. C. Bifield and his wife took over the *Three Crowns* inn and encouraged day-trippers. This picture of 1930 shows a sedate group of open-air enthusiasts enjoying the sea-breezes. The landlord, Mr. Bifield, is standing in the doorway.

84. This picture shows the *Three Crowns* on Whit Monday 1926. Those queuing for teas wait at the back door whilst those wanting something stronger queue at the front. In the foreground families can be seen enjoying the 'beach'.

85. Behind the *Three Crowns* a driver and two conductors take a stroll. Buses are said to have served the *Three Crowns* until 1961. This picture was probably taken from one of the inn's windows by Mr. Bifield.

86.   The Crowns football team, 1934.

87.   Mr. and Mrs. Bifield outside the inn with some of their patrons. Note the flag; the date on the photograph is 1935 which suggests that it might be flying in celebration of George V's jubilee.

88.   Mr. and Mrs. Bifield and family celebrate 13 years' tenancy of the inn. A board proclaims 1923-36. The children on the 'beach' seem to be enjoying the occasion.

89. Brights Farmhouse which stood along Upminster Road South. The road still curves slightly where it had once to avoid the pond.

90. Charlotte's Alley, though picturesque, is representative of the less than ideal accommodation of many Rainham residents. These weather-boarded cottages stood on the site of the present driveway between the library and the Family Centre. The cottages were demolished in 1940 but the pump remained for some years.

91. Rainham Village Brass Band, 1910.

92. Rainham Working Men's Silver Prize Band marching through Aveley village in 1937.

93. The Rainham marshes provided an ideal location for the sport of coursing. These greyhounds are being prepared at Whybridge kennels, South Hornchurch.

94. George Rogers (1845-1906), seen posing here in a photographer's studio, was gamekeeper to the South Essex Coursing Club which was based at Rainham.

95. The *Lennard Arms*, Wennington, seen here in 1914. Before 1823 it was known as the *Crown and Cushion*. In the 18th century the parish vestrymen had a celebratory meal here at Christmas and Easter, paid for from the rates. At the turn of the century the *Essex Weekly News* stated that the pub was a few yards outside the Wennington boundary, coming within the parish of Aveley.

96. A photograph of the *Cauliflower* before its rebuilding in 1907. It began as a beerhouse in a converted cottage in 1878. Farmer E. Blewitt founded the business, giving it a name appropriate to its surroundings, for it was at one time surrounded by market gardens.

97. Children playing in Back Street (now Upminster Road South) *c.*1900. This picture looks eastwards towards the church.

98. Children skipping in front of some large sawn tree trunks in Back Street, *c.*1900. The *Cauliflower* inn sign can be seen in the background.

Chariots of Progress

99. A page from *Paterson's Roads* 18th edition, 1822. At the beginning of the 19th century crossroads at what is now the very busy Dovers corner did not exist. There were no roads westwards to the *Chequers*, Dagenham or eastwards to the *Lennard Arms*. Traffic from Rainham went via Dovers Farm to the *Cherry Tree*, along the only London road, then going via Ilford and Stratford. The Napoleonic wars ensured that a direct route to Tilbury Fort was constructed; this new turnpike used Ripple Road and a new road (it still bears this name) between the *Chequers* and Dovers Farm was built. The road then turned south onto the existing road, through Rainham and Wennington. The London to Tilbury journey was thus shortened from 29 to 22 miles.

MEASURED from WHITECHAPEL CHURCH | LONDON TO SOUTHEND, WITH A BRANCH TO TILBURY FORT. | THROUGH BARKING, RAINHAM, STANFORD LE HOPE, and HADLEIGH

but its consequence in after-times was certainly owing to an abbey, which is said to have been the first convent for women established in this kingdom: scarcely any vestiges of the buildings are, however, now in existence, though the site of the abbey-church may still be seen just without the north wall of the present church-yard, at the entrance to which there is an ancient square embattled gateway, with octagonal turrets, also embattled, rising from the ground on each side. The town is situated on the river Roding, commonly called Barking creek, which, about two miles lower down, runs into the Thames, from whence various articles are brought up in vessels for the supply of the adjacent country. It is principally inhabited by fishermen, has a weekly market on Saturday, and contains a spacious and convenient work-house, a penitentiary on Howard's plan, a market-house, and a parochial church, which latter building is dedicated to St. Margaret, and has a square embattled tower at the west end: it contains a number of monuments, but particularly one against the south wall of the chancel, to the memory of Sir Charles Montague, brother of the first Earl of Manchester, who died in the year 1625. Barking and its neighbourhood supplies the London markets with vast quantities of vegetables, particularly potatoes, the profits arising from the growth of which are considerable, as the produce is abundant, owing to the mode of cultivation, and the excellent quality of the soil.

BEAM BRIDGE. Ford House, *Christopher Tyler*, Esq.

WINNINGTON, 1¼ m. beyond, Bell House, Sir *Thos. Barret Lennard*, Bart.

STIFFORD BRIDGE. Ford Place, *Zach. Button*, Esq.; a little farther, The Parsonage, Rev. Dr. *Hogarth;* Corbet Hall, *Philip Button*, Esq.; and Stifford Lodge, *John Button*, Esq.

BAKER STREET. 1 m. distant, at Orset, The Rectory, Rev. *John Frederick Uske.*

COCK ALEHOUSE, see at a distance, Thorndon Hall, Lord *Petre*. This magnificent seat stands on a fine eminence in an extensive park, at the south extremity of an avenue leading from Brentwood; it was erected from designs by, and under the direction of, Paine; it is built with white brick; and consists of a centre, connected to two wings by circular corridors, and having on the north side a portico resting on six fluted Corinthian pillars. The roof of the hall, a noble room 40 feet square, is supported by 18 columns, covered with a composition resembling marble; the drawing-room, 38 feet by 26, is hung with green damask; the library, a

From Southend		From London
	Cross the river Lea, and enter Essex.	
$33\frac{3}{4}$	East Ham, *Essex*	6
	Cross the river Roding	
$32\frac{3}{4}$	*BARKING*	7
$29\frac{1}{2}$	The Chequers, *Division of the Road*	$10\frac{1}{4}$
	to Dagenham 1 m.	
	$\frac{1}{4}$ m. farther,	
	to Dagenham 1 m.	
29	Beam River Turnpike	$10\frac{3}{4}$
$28\frac{3}{4}$	Beam Bridge	11
	Cross the river Beam	
	Entrance of Rainham,	
	to Romford $4\frac{3}{4}$ m.	
$27\frac{1}{4}$	*To* * Rainham, *Church*	$12\frac{1}{2}$
26	Winnington, *Church*	$13\frac{3}{4}$
$25\frac{1}{2}$	Junction of the Road	$14\frac{1}{4}$
	Forward to Purfleet $1\frac{1}{4}$ m.	
$23\frac{3}{4}$	*to* Aveley, *Church*	16
	Before Stifford Bridge,	
	to Romford 9 m.	
22	Stifford Bridge	$17\frac{3}{4}$
$21\frac{1}{2}$	Dog and Partridge	$18\frac{1}{4}$
$21\frac{1}{4}$	Stifford, *Church*	$18\frac{1}{2}$
	To Grays Thurrock 2 m.	
19	Baker Street	$20\frac{3}{4}$
	Forward to Orset $\frac{3}{4}$ m.	
$18\frac{1}{2}$	*To* Division of the Road	$21\frac{1}{4}$
	Forward to Tilbury Fort 4 m.	
	London to Tilbury Fort $25\frac{1}{4}$ *m.*	
$17\frac{1}{4}$	*to* Cock Alehouse	$22\frac{1}{2}$
	to Brentwood 9 m.	
	$1\frac{1}{2}$ m. farther,	
	To Tilbury Fort $4\frac{1}{2}$ m.	
$15\frac{3}{4}$	Junction of the Road	24
	to Horndon on the Hill $\frac{3}{4}$ m., thence to Billericay $7\frac{1}{2}$ m.	
$15\frac{1}{4}$	Stanford le Hope, *King's Head*	$24\frac{1}{2}$
$11\frac{1}{2}$	Vange, *Church*	$28\frac{1}{4}$
$9\frac{3}{4}$	Pitsey, *Church*	30
9	Bowers, *The Gun*	$30\frac{3}{4}$
$6\frac{1}{2}$	Jarvis Hill, *top of*	$33\frac{1}{4}$

the expense of 1,200,000*l*. by a company of private individuals. Beyond the above, at the eastern extremity of Blackwall, are situated the East India Docks: these had also their origin about the beginning of the present century, and were constructed at the expense of the East India Company.

BARKING, 1 m. beyond, Eastbury House, *unoccupied*. This ancient brick structure is supposed to have been erected by Sir W. Denham, to whom Edward VI. granted the estate: it has octangular towers and curiously ornamental chimneys; some of the apartments are also painted in fresco. This mansion is traditionally associated with the gunpowder-plot, one account asserting that the conspirators here held their meetings; and another that it was the residence of Lord Monteagle when he received the letter that led to the discovery.—— Between Barking and Rainham, see, across the Thames, Belvedere, Lord *Say* and *Sele*.

WINNINGTON. *W. Warren*, Esq.

STIFFORD, 1¼ m. distant, Belmont Castle, *Richard Webb*, Esq.

BAKER STREET, beyond, — *Newcomb*, Esq.

JARVIS HILL. From the summit of this hill a most delightful prospect is obtained over the river Thames, which is here seen to singular advantage spreading its expansive bosom for many miles in extent, continually enlivened by the numerous vessels which are constantly navigating this important portion of the noblest river in the world; while the scene is rendered truly enchanting by the broken range of the coast of Kent, whose undulating surface, clothed with the softest verdure, and bespangled with flourishing villages, forms a sylvan back-ground to the view; the whole presenting to the enraptured eye of the spectator a combination of beauties rarely to be met with.

HADLEIGH TURNPIKE. Hadleigh Hall, Rev. Sir *John Head*, Bart.

SOUTHEND is eligibly situated on the acclivity of a well-wooded hill, at the mouth of the Thames, nearly opposite to Sheerness; it has within these few years obtained some repute as a bathing-place, and has since continued to rise in importance: the soil is sandy, and the shore flat and shallow, but at full tide the view is admirable; the air is dry and salubrious, and the water, notwithstanding its mixture with the Thames, is clear and salt: besides the machines, which are neat and commodious, here are two warm-baths. The terrace, commonly called New Southend, stands on a considerable eminence, and is a handsome range of buildings, finished

Railway Station, Southend

100. The London, Tilbury and Southend Railway came to Barking and Dagenham in April 1854. In March 1856 it reached Southend; this engraving shows the first station at Southend. Dagenham Dock station was not opened until July 1908.

101. Many cheap excursions to Southend and other resorts were run from local stations at Bank Holidays. This leaflet advertises such a trip for August Bank Holiday 1905.

...on Tilbury and Southend Railway.

BANK HOLIDAYS. *5.8.05*

On Sunday, 6th & Monday, 7th August,

CHEAP EXCURSION TICKETS

FOR

SOUTHEND

AND

WESTCLIFF-on-SEA,

WILL BE ISSUED AT

ROMFORD,

DAGENHAM, HORNCHURCH,

UPMINSTER,

OCKENDON,

GRAYS,

AND

GRAVESEND,

(TOWN PIER)

BY ALL TRAINS.

Fares for the Double Journey—

FROM	1st Class.	3rd Class.
ROMFORD (L.T. & S.R. Station)	4/-	2/-
DAGENHAM	3/6	1/9
HORNCHURCH		
UPMINSTER		
OCKENDON	3/-	1/6
GRAYS or GRAVESEND ...		

The Tickets issued at Dagenham, Hornchurch, Upminster, Ockendon, Grays and Gravesend, will be available for the Return Journey on the day of issue only.

FENCHURCH ST. TERMINUS.
July, 1905.

ARTHUR L. STRIDE,
Managing Director.

Daniel Greenaway & Sons, Printers, London, E.C.

102. Rainham's early wooden station was elevated above the marshland, but in January 1891 the whole of the down platform, including the booking office and two waiting rooms, were burnt down. This picture shows the rebuilt station *c.*1898, which was a wooden structure.

103. The original signalbox, *c.*1912.

104. The London, Tilbury and Southend Railway kept their engines in immaculate condition. This is their six-coupled Radial Tank locomotive no. 69. The destination, Gravesend, was, of course, not reached by train but by ferry from Tilbury Riverside.

L. T. & S. R. "Corringham."
Six Coupled Radial Tank Locomotive. No. 69.

105. Dagenham Dock station being built, 1908.

106. Dagenham station on the Barking - Pitsea line opened in May 1885. It was the nearest station to the old village.

107. Dagenham station platforms, *c.*1906.

108. A locomotive in 1959 hauls a train into Rainham station. The station has changed little since its construction in 1898, retaining the wooden station building and overbridge.

109. In 1909 this wooden hanger was built by the Dagenham builders West and Coe to house a captive balloon used in early experiments by the Royal Aeronautical Society on their Dagenham Dock flying ground, close to where Ford's gatehouse later stood.

110. Walter Howgego's first motor cars seen at the Bull Corner, close to his Dagenham shop.

111. New Road, Dagenham before the advent of the motor car. The road was built during the Napoleonic wars to cater for military traffic going to Tilbury Fort. Motor traffic was eventually to become a nuisance to the inhabitants of the rows of cottages.

112. Mr. Edwards provided transport for Rainham before the buses served the distant parts of the village. He also ran buses to the *Three Crowns* on the riverbank.

113. A summer scene at the *Bull Inn*, *c.*1922 with the first bus to provide Dagenham with a service (National route N20) on the right. The bus advertises Dunlop tyres, Neaves Food for Babies and Maples furniture. Notice the bicycle temporarily parked behind the tall 'stink' (ventilation) pipe. The bus driver is wearing the all white uniform that was common in the 1920s and '30s.

114.   A 1924 solid-tyred General bus on route 23A waits at the bus stand next to Rainham war memorial prior to leaving for Marylebone station.

115. A list of bus routes serving Dagenham and Rainham.

23 Sundays Service 12 mins Fare 1/3	**WORMWOOD SCRUBS** Via North Pole Rd, St. Quintin Avenue, Westbourne Grove, Marble Arch, Bank, C'm'rc'l Rd Barking **DAGENHAM** Time 112 mins
23 W'kdays Service 4 mins Fare 1/-	**MARYLEBONE STN.** Via Baker Street thence as Sunday Route to **DAGENHAM** Time 103 mins Service: Dag'ham 15 mins Barking 4 mins
A 23 Sundays Service 12 mins Fare 1/5	**WORMWOOD SCRUBS** Via same as Route 23 to Dagenham thence via Ripple Rd, Dagenham Marsh **RAINHAM** Time 125 mins
A 23 W'kdays Service 60 mins Fare 1/2	**MARYLEBONE STN.** (G.C.R.) Via Baker St, thence as Sunday Route **RAINHAM** Time 116 mins

115. A list of bus routes serving Dagenham and Rainham.

116. Heathway from Oxlow Lane, June 1925. Children play in the litter-free streets, whilst the man on the right may be seen reaching for the key to his 'modern' house. Only one bus is visible – not a car or van in sight.

117.   An outing for ladies and children is about to set out from Becontree Heath post office. Wheal and Crane of Ilford have supplied one large charabanc and a smaller one to convey the party.

118.   Outside the *Chequers* public house in the 1930s. Three white-coated bus drivers can be seen – one at the wheel of the bus approaching from the Rainham direction.

119. The network of the bus service in 1934. Note that Dagenham stadium is marked, this presumably provided a great source of revenue on dog-racing nights.

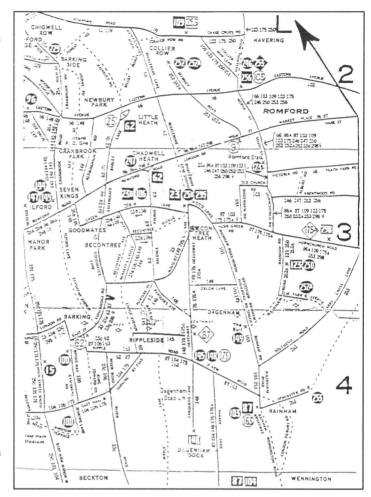

120. A Green Line coach on the Z1 route which ran from London to Dagenham, Rainham and Grays is seen here at the Aldgate terminus. Green Line coach services provided a more efficient form of travel in the late 1930s, with limited stops and comfortable interiors.

The New Century Dawns

121. At a glance, this view of Bull Street, Dagenham, could have been taken at the turn of the century. Closer inspection, however, shows a car in Howgego's yard waiting to emerge into the street, although the clearance on either side of the car appears very narrow. The passenger in the car could be Mrs. Prosser-Evans.

122. A close-up of the converted house where parish council business was transacted and rates were paid. The office was very convenient for Dagenham village but with the construction of the Becontree estate it was no longer central and was subsequently abandoned in 1926.

123. A class photo from Dagenham village school, *c*,1911. There are twice as many boys as girls; the First World War, however, was soon to turn such an imbalance around, with many older pupils being claimed as casualties.

124. W. H. Arthy's bakery in Crown Street is seen here decorated for the carnival, *c*.1910.

125. The railway branch lines into Dagenham dock. Samuel Williams purchased this large area of land in 1887 after previous schemes had run out of capital. When Williams first took over there was only a rail line ending on a wooden jetty, everything else – houses, water supply, light and power – had to be provided from scratch.

126. It is true to say that the conversion of Dagenham dock from barren land into a thriving business was little short of a miracle. Even the land itself needed to be built up from the marsh before any buildings could be erected. However, by 1911 the company had the facilities to receive the last great ship constructed on the River Thames, H.M.S. *Thunderer*, which was built at the Thames Ironworks up the river. It was towed to a specially constructed deep-water jetty which had taken only nine months to complete. In addition a 150-ton floating crane was brought down the river. This picture shows H.M.S. *Thunderer* leaving the jetty in March 1912. Since that date the jetty has always been known as the *Thunderer*.

127. H.M.S. *Thunderer* was to prove an unlucky ship, being lost with all hands in the Battle of Jutland. The docks prospered, however, with much of the reclaimed land being developed as an industrial estate. Before the outbreak of war in 1914 four new factories had been built and leased to tenants. After the war many new factories were constructed on piled foundations, special pile casting beds being laid at the dock for this. The results of the transformation of this area are seen here in 1928.

128. Although Rainham's Broadway retains its basic shape it is hard to believe that it looked like this in 1898. For a main road the surface is very primitive. The storage building next to the *Angel* and the bank of the Ingrebourne can be seen in this unusual perspective view.

129. By 1905 the scene had changed. Many more shopping facilities now existed, with a variety of shops in the central block, Joslin's tea and dining rooms catered for visitors, advertising specially for those involved in the cycling craze.

130. At the beginning of the 20th century the *Three Crowns* had become a pub serving factory workers, rather than the travellers and ferry users of earlier times. The first industries in the area created a small hamlet known as Back Way, which had its own general store, the Little Wonder. The first industry on the marsh dated from 1869 and in 1873 Miller and Johnson built a manure works. Fields candle makers turned to making explosives during the First World War, but blew up in 1917. In the same year Murex came to the area, and over the years took over all the factory space, eventually absorbing the inn.

131. A 1920s view of Rainham's industrial riverside. Hempleman's 185-ft. chimney stack of 1908 dominates the other factory buildings which were originally used for the manufacture of fertiliser. The black wooden house, the last on the riverbank, was used by Murex as company offices upon their arrival in 1917.

132. White's mooring barge, the *Old Elizabeth*, built in 1824.

133. At the turn of the century this field was where St Helen's Court (off Upminster Road South) now stands.

134. On the other side of Upminster Road South was the Hollies. This picture dates from the early 1900s.

135. This saddler's shop was situated in Rainham village. It later became Wisbeys then Cutbush's. The men are dressed up in their best for a special occasion. It is quite likely, however, that Artie Cook (second from right) would soon be in hot water, as apparently 'trouble was his second name'!

136. Parsons' tailor's shop in the Broadway has an
elaborately styled fascia. The sign-board on the right is also
quite florid and advertises a fire and life insurance company
with its head office in Cheapside.

137. Rainham's brick war memorial, now usually referred to
as the clock tower, was unveiled in 1921 by the Lord
Lieutenant of Essex, Sir Francis Whitmore. The memorial,
which has three clock faces, is seen here decorated with
wreaths for an Armistice Day remembrance. The site on
which the memorial stands was originally known as the
Green.

138. Wooden palings surround the villas in Cowper Road. The dress of the women suggests that the picture was taken on a Sunday morning.

139. 7 Devonshire Terrace, a private dwelling, housed the first telephone exchange for Rainham. It was opened in 1899, and by 1 January 1909 still had only eight lines!

140. Chas Fuller, the Dagenham village harness-maker stands at the door of his Bull Street shop in 1923. The business had been taken over from a member of the West family. Edward West, saddler, appears in a trade directory of 1866.

141. The last of Becontree Heath, 1930. An old barn on the boundary of the Heath links old and new by displaying posters for Bovril, Combes Brown Ale and the latest offering at the Regent Cinema, *The Love Parade*. On the left sewer pipes are being laid.

142. Washing day at Becontree Heath, 1930, almost certainly a Monday. By the lamp post surveying work is in progress, in preparation for the enclosure of the Heath.

'And Build a City Here'

143. Becontree estate during construction. Looking at the backs of the houses in Northfield Road, June 1929.

144. One of the many churches built to serve the new Becontree estate was the Roman Catholic St Vincent's. The house on the left was for the priest. This picture dates from 1934.

145. Attractions on the new estate, the *Royal Oak*, Green Lane whilst at the Heathway shopping centre the cinema is showing *The Bishop's Wife*, starring Cary Grant.

146. Valence Avenue, *c.*1930.

The "Servall" GRATE

A Sitting-Room Fire with all the services of a Kitchen Range.

Roomy Oven, Large Hobs, H. P. Boiler giving always plentiful Hot Water.

Brickwork Opening **14 in. Only**

Grate is made in various Settings and Finishes.

Ask your Merchants for Illustrated Price Lists or send direct to the makers . .

The Coalbrookdale Company Ltd., Coalbrookdale, Shropshire.

147. Advertising material of the 1920s aimed at estate dwellers.

148. Becontree Avenue with its parade of shops was built to cater for the new estate dwellers. On the right a 'flivver' has stopped to allow a conversation to take place. The gardens down the middle of the estate's avenues were originally occupied by the building contractor's railways which brought materials to the green field site.

149. The gentle curve of Oxlow Lane relieves the tedium of the straight lines that were common on the estate. The facilities provided here include another shopping parade and the Beacon off-licence. This picture dates from the 1930s.

150. Sterling's Radio factory, Dagenham, provided employment for those living in the original village and the new estate.

151. Terrace View in the late 1920s; a view of factories was inevitable in some parts of the estate.

152. The inter-war development of Rainham owes much to the homestead or plotland idea. Many East Londoners and others bought plots of land at Rainham, travelling out at weekends to build houses or bungalows on them. Building provided a leisure occupation and holiday activity as well as the ultimate goal of home ownership. Of course, many owners lost enthusiasm and lots of homes were never properly completed. Many of the roads were also not paved until well after the Second World War. This photograph shows a scene on the Parsonage estate, Upminster Road North, *c.*1923. The houses on the right were destroyed by enemy action during the Second World War.

153. Hubert Road in the 1920s showing the typical style of dwelling built on these 'laissez faire' developments.

154. No look at Dagenham can ignore the nationally known Girl Pipers. As can be seen from this and the following three photographs, which were issued as postcards by their founder, the Congregational Minister, the Rev. J. W. Graves, there were even early international contacts. The pipers have provided not only enjoyment but musical training and discipline for several generations of Dagenham girls, since the group's first practice on Saturday 4 October 1930.

Menin Gate, Ypres.

Tyne Kot British Cemetery.

DAGENHAM GIRL PIPERS ON TOUR IN BELGIUM, 1933.

A Scene in Bruges.

England Once More.

Copyright
Rev. J. W. Graves,
December.

155. The old Rainham school building of 1872.

156. John Wesley cottages were believed to be some of the oldest dwellings in Rainham. It is said that Wesley, the great religious leader, gained inspiration for writing whilst staying here.

157. Chandler's Corner on the corner of the Southend road became well known as a landmark for obtaining traffic reports and road directions. This shows a view of the shop and various traffic signals.

158. Pictured here *c.*1963, is the cottage with the porch, which stood next to the *Phoenix Inn* and served as Mayhew's butcher's shop. Following demolition in 1964, a modern building was erected by Stanton Radio and this was converted into Rainham library which opened in 1967.

159. Another building that lingered into modern times was Waterman's Cottage, which belonged to Jack Keys. This is a rear view taken in 1934.

160. Rainham Lodge was on the borders of the parishes of Hornchurch and Upminster, but it lay within Rainham. It was the birthplace of a famous son of Rainham, Baron Strang, diplomat and author. The house was demolished in 1960.

161. Did you say 'Build a factory here'? Major Holman, representing Ford's architects, looks rather aghast standing amongst the vegetation of the proposed new factory site.

162. Another view of the remote stretch of land that was to become Ford's. Trenthams the contractors were to make their name converting 330 acres over a three-year period into a modern industrial complex.

163. The life-style and habits of the navvy did not change much in a century. On this site, between 1929-31, however, they were engaged in a revolutionary task. Hard bouts of physical labour were interspersed with tea-breaks.

164. Baulks of timber are positioned, whilst the steam pile-drivers stand by.

165. A skip containing a load of concrete is steadied. It will later be poured into the foundations of a factory building which will become the by-products plant.

166. Protruding from the ground are some of the thousands of steel-reinforced concrete piles upon which the Ford plant is built. A steam piling rig stands in front of nearly completed buildings. First Williams and secondly Trentham's transformed the face of the marshland within 50 years.

167. The Ford plant from the air showing the impressive acreage and the jetty facilities on the Thames.

168a. The factory in production, casting pig-iron.

168b. Men at work on a battery of presses.

168c. A discharging coke oven.

169. One of the beautifully maintained locomotives on the rail complex inside the works.

170. A party at Dorothy Barley school, Dagenham, 1937. It was probably held to celebrate the Coronation. Looking at the children's faces it seems a serious affair, but they may have been overawed by the presence of a photographer. Sylvia Mansfield is the girl pupil second left.

171. A class photograph of Rainham infants school, Upminster Road, *c.*1949.

172. Dagenham Urban District Council made use of an old army hut for a public library. In spite of the somewhat humble location, the librarian, with considerable flair, invited Dr. Arundell Esdaile from the British Museum to perform the opening ceremony on 10 May 1930.

173. Rainham's shop library (shop premises converted to use as libraries usually in commercial areas) this was replaced in the 1960s by the present building which had been adapted from business use.

174. Rainham's fire brigade pose neatly around their new fire engine in 1933. The turnout is superintended by Captain Layzell, the man in the centre of the three standing on the engine. Second Officer, J. Swann, stands by the front wheel. The men are all part-time fire fighters.

175. Rainham fire brigade was formed in 1904 and disbanded in 1936, being absorbed by the Hornchurch fire brigade. This corrugated iron shed at the corner of Parkway served as the fire station. The drying tower, siren and alarm can all be seen.

176. An impressive turnout of vehicles at Dagenham urban district council's fire and ambulance station, Becontree Heath, 1930.

177. Industrial premises on Ripple Road in the 1930s. A modern fire brigade was essential in an area such as Dagenham which had numerous industrial premises and factories.

178. The Second World War on Thameside. One hundred and seventy battery firing its 4.5-in. guns from the Aylett's Farm site in Rainham. From right to left the guns are numbers 2 and 3 whilst the flash from number 4 can be also be seen. Also to the far right of the picture is part of the command post and to the left of number 2 gun is the battery trolley that was used to transport the huge battery that operated the power rammer in the loading tray. A Mr. R. Harris was in number 3 gun, with a consignment of 17-and 18-year-olds, known as the 'Immatures', who came from the Devon, Somerset, Dorset, Wiltshire and Kent Yeomanry Regiments to serve with this and similar batteries.

179. There were still contrasts between the old and new, even in the Dagenham of 1932. This picture was captioned 'Power, ancient and modern – plough horses passing one of the new pylons forming part of the electrical scheme of the district'.

'80. Rainham Road, the right-hand side of the new Dagenham Civic Centre, may be seen, together with the tower and main block of the new fire station, opened in 1937. An efficient system of highway lighting occupies the central reservation.

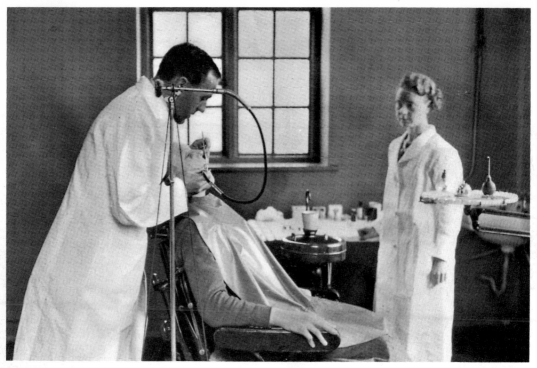

181. Dental services were provided in one of the six clinics which catered for the Dagenham district in the late 1930s. The facilities shown here were amongst the most modern in Britain at the time.

182. Before the advent of the National Health Service various schemes were organised for people who were ill. The Dagenham and District Nursing Association was one such scheme. It provided paid up members with 'a fully qualified nurse in times of Sickness'.

EXTRACTS FROM RULES.

1.—A Member is not entitled to benefits until contributions have been paid over a period of three months.

2.—Members who are more than three months in arrears are not entitled to benefits and will be charged for attendance as if they were non-members.

3.—Except in the case of a first visit, the Nurse's services will only be available where the case is under the care of a Doctor.

4.—Should the Nurse advise the calling in of a Doctor and her advice be disregarded, the Nurse shall not attend the patient except in case of fresh emergency. The Nurse shall report such case to the Secretary.

5.—Application for a visit should be made to the Nurse before 8.30 a.m. for morning visit or before 4.30 p.m. for an evening visit except in cases of emergency.

6.—Except in cases of emergency night duty is not undertaken and only serious cases will be attended on Sundays.

7.—No dressings or medicine are supplied.

8.—This card must be produced to the Visiting Nurse at her first visit and thereafter as required.

9.—A Meeting of Members will be held annually to elect the Committee and Officers.

per Mrs Dunham

DAGENHAM DISTRICT NURSING ASSOCIATION

In affiliation with the Queen's Institute of District Nursing.

Contributions.—4/4 per annum (minimum), which covers the contributor and all **DEPENDANTS.** Those whose income is more than 15s. and less than 30s., 2/2 per annum.

Benefits.—A fully qualified Visiting Nurse in times of Sickness.

Applications for a Nurse should be made to:

Organising Secretary for Contributory Scheme,

TELEPHONE **York House,**
SEVEN KINGS 2760. **Frizlands Lane.**

Group _____ C·/4/.
Total Contributions _____ 4/4· Arrears _____
Date of Joining _____ 5/8/41
Date of issue of this Card _____ 13/8/41
NAME _____ Miss D. Rackham.
ADDRESS _____ 56. Albany Rd
Chadwell Heath

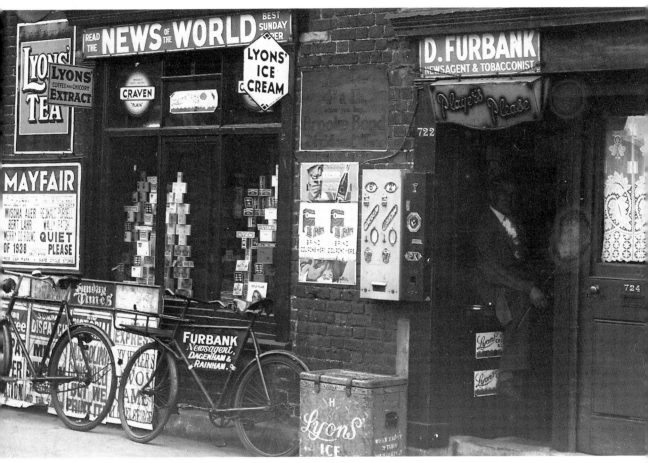

183. The general stores opposite the White House in Bull Street, Dagenham, *c.*1947. This picture is indicative of the early post-war years when Britain tried to recover from its huge war effort. In spite of the lack of colour in the home and on the streets (most cars were black), shortages in nearly all commodities and other privations, these were good years to grow up in. Most people were cheerfully 'making do and mending' or doing without, glad that the war was finally over.

184. Envoi, Rainham 1957. By the late 1950s things were definitely getting better throughout the country. The economy was improving and people's lives were becoming more colourful again. In addition, during the war most people had become more international in their outlook. An interest in culture and the arts was developing, and the country was on the verge of a revolution in Youth Culture as the post-war generation prospered.